I0480417

Working from home

Earn money online, start a side-hustle, take control of your life and become a successful entrepreneur

Uwe Sawinski

Table of contents

Introduction

Working from home seems to be a dream for most of us. However, many working people don't realize how easy it actually is to leave employment and earn money from home. Activities carried out from home can take many different forms. You can become self-employed or work as a freelancer, you can take so-called remote jobs or simply pursue your permanent employment in a home office. In this book, I would like to show you the different types of work you can do from home. I would like to concentrate with you on freelance and commercial activities.

Over the last years I could gain a lot of experience in this area and would like to give you now in this book practical tips that will enable you soon to realize your dream of no longer having to rely on someone else to earn your own money.

Being able to work from home has many advantages. You no longer have to drive to work every morning, you can get up when you want to, and have the freedom to manage your own time. You will have the freedom to spend time with your children or partner when you want to or to take breaks when you really need them. And most importantly, you will have the freedom to not have to listen to anyone else.

Once you have enjoyed this freedom, you will not want to lose it again. On the other hand, people who have never had this freedom will find it hard to understand this feeling.

Every beginning will be difficult. Not everything is going to go your way. Especially the first months of your independence will be full of challenges and problems. However, once you have survived this time, nothing will throw you off track so quickly and you will face new challenges with determination.

I hope that this book will not only give you practical tips, but also help you to overcome your fear. You have nothing to fear. And if you should make a mistake once, then get up again and continue. Many successful entrepreneurs have already failed. The difference between a successful entrepreneur and a person who returns to employment after the first failure is that the successful entrepreneur has not let himself be brought down. The successful entrepreneur saw the setbacks as an opportunity to grow and do better next time. Because one day the day will come when you wake up and know that you have made it. You have fulfilled your dream and can now live self-determinedly according to your own rules. Such a dream is worth fighting for.

But first of all I wish you a lot of fun reading this book and hope that you will soon be able to start your own business.

CHAPTER 1: Start into self-employment

Start your own business: Are you ready?

Are you ready to be self-employed and work independently? If you work from home, no one will tell you what to do and which tasks need to be done by the end of the day. This is something you have to do from now on.

Before you work from home or start your own business, you should think about whether you want to do this at all. Many people have no problem working for someone else. You will receive your salary every month, you don't have to insure yourself and if you get sick, you will continue to receive at least part of your salary. In addition, many people really enjoy having a clear daily routine and knowing that new tasks are waiting for them every day. All this could be missing if you work from home.

Think back into the past and consider whether there have been times when you have been completely on your own. Were you able to motivate yourself to take a step forward every day and take on tasks or did you just not get along with such situations until now? Be honest with yourself. You can still reject your decision. An independent lifestyle is not for everyone. You will have to shoulder the entire risk for your own well-being and possibly the well-being of the people around you, for example your children or parents. Many break under this pressure. The best thing to do would therefore be to start earning some money online in addition to your current employment. You are testing your own abilities and proving to yourself that you have what it takes to earn your own money. If you decide to become an entrepreneur, at least you have the certainty that you don't have to start from scratch, but have already had your first successful experiences. If your employer doesn't allow you to earn money besides your job, you should save up a buffer of at least six months' salary to be able to start your entrepreneurial career successfully.

Before you start your business, however, you should first find a profitable business idea. The following three factors are especially important in order to find a profitable business idea:

Develop a business idea: Finding a good business idea is not easy. As a rule of thumb, however, you can remember that a good product or service always solves the customers' problems. In addition, you should always consider the supply and demand for your product or service. Ideally, you should develop a business idea for a product for which there is a lot of demand but no supply. However, such business ideas are very rare and often these types of business ideas require a lot of capital. You don't always have to be the first on the market to make a lot of money with your idea. And if you don't want to earn tens of thousands of Euros a month, almost every business idea can improve your financial situation. Make sure that your business idea fits you. Many founders find out about business ideas from other entrepreneurs in whom they have confidence. However, if other people implement a business idea and earn their money with it, this does not mean that you can do the same. So be sure that your business idea really fits you. You can ensure this by analysing your strengths and weaknesses. Are you perhaps a born salesman or are you perhaps rather introverted? Are you a technical genius and should concentrate completely on product development or are you more the manager and planner who manages to turn visions into reality with the help of others? Once you have found an answer, you should compare your strengths and weaknesses with the business ideas you have developed so far and find that there are matches or no matches with the business ideas.

Longevity of the business idea: It is also crucial that you develop a business idea that will continue to be profitable for years to come. Let's say, for example, that you want to open a CD shop. Nowadays, hardly anyone buys CDs in a shop. Most likely, this trend will decrease even more, so that in a few years you won't be able to make any money with such a business idea. So keep in mind that many business ideas will not be profitable forever. Every business will disappear one day. Your task is to change yourself daily, to offer new products and services and to keep up with the times.

Proof of the profitability of the business idea: It is also crucial that your business idea actually works. Now that you have already come up with a business idea that suits you, you should also find out whether this business idea is actually profitable. See if other people have already made money with this idea. If you consider yourself to be as talented as these people, you can assume that you will have similar success with the business idea. If you know from several sources that a certain business idea or source of income is worthwhile, you can assume that it will be worthwhile for you.

The 8 skills of successful entrepreneurs

Working successfully from home is not easy. Many entrepreneurs fail to work from home for long periods of time because they cannot motivate themselves, do not take care of their own bookkeeping properly or simply because they do not have a talent for sales. However, these are only some of the skills needed to become a successful entrepreneur. In the following, I would like to introduce you to eight important skills that you need to be able to work successfully from home.

1. Organization: It will be crucial for your success that you are able to organize yourself. Especially if you decide to register a business or choose the freelancer status, you will have to do accounting tasks in addition to customer acquisition, completing tasks, writing emails and answering questions. This is exactly why it is important that you can organize yourself. Good organisation starts with order. Make sure that your workplace is tidy and clearly structured. Especially if you have many customers, it can be advantageous to work without paper. Your workplace should be minimalist and

there should be nothing on the table that you don't need for your work. To keep your table clean throughout the day, it is recommended to clean it up once a day, preferably at the end of the day, and prepare it for the next day. It is also important that you can arrange your tasks correctly. Some tasks should be given priority, other tasks can be postponed. However, your customers also expect high quality results from you. So don't let them wait too long for their results. Every morning, make a list of the tasks that need to be done today. Also make a note of when you have accepted certain orders and when these orders have to be completed. You may also find it useful to prepare a daily to-do list that you can use as a guide throughout the day. This list should be a help for you and show you which tasks you still have to do and which you have already completed.

In order to be able to create such to-do lists, however, you should be able to assess yourself objectively. Only if you can assess yourself, you will be able to achieve the goals you have defined. If you can't assess yourself, you will always achieve less than you set out to do or achieve more without ever being able to fully exploit your own potential.

However, not only task lists are important, but also clearly defined limits. You also need breaks. So define for yourself when you take a break. This includes explicit breaks between work hours and whole days every week or every few weeks when you don't think about your work.

Organization also plays a big role when it comes to accounting and taxes. If you become self-employed or work on a freelance basis, you will also have to deal with occasional accounting tasks. And you should not underestimate these. A good organization is essential here. Before you start your own business, it is best to take an accounting course to learn how to sort out your accounting tasks, which registrations have to be made and when which documents have to be submitted. Mistakes in this regard can unfortunately be expensive and lead to unpleasant consequences. For this very reason, accounting should be one of the first things you should learn before you start.

2. Self-assessment: Self-assessment is very important if you want to work from home. You can optimize your ability to assess yourself objectively by defining goals on a daily basis and try to achieve them with all your strength. If you do not achieve these goals, you know that you have overestimated yourself. If you reach these goals and you have a lot of time left over that you would normally have used to reach the goal, then you know that you have underestimated yourself. Only when you reach your goals without having much excess time at the end of the day, you know that you can judge yourself well. Train this ability every day. You will be amazed at what you will be able to do or you will realize that you have completely overestimated yourself.

It can also be helpful to talk to other people and ask them how they see your work. And whether the opinions of others agree with what you thought of yourself. It often hurts us when other people think about us differently than we think about ourselves. In such situations, however, you should leave your feelings outside and concentrate only on what will help you personally. And this includes the honest opinion of your friends, acquaintances, customers or even perhaps family members.

3. Self-motivation: Motivating oneself is not very easy for many people. Many things seem to hold us back every day and we allow doubts to arise. We don't believe that we have the talent or ability to achieve certain goals, but we are surprised when other people do. Most of us underestimate what we are capable of.

If you want to work successfully from home, you should have the ability to motivate yourself. This ability can be learned and develops over time. However, if you can't motivate yourself at all and can't do things yourself, then this activity might not be for you.

A big problem that you will soon face is distractions. Most of us feel very comfortable in our own homes. But this does not only have advantages. Typical distractions are the television, e-mails, social media notifications or other people. There is nothing wrong with distractions, but you should try to minimize them during your working hours. How to do this is explained later in this book.

4. Flexibility: You need to be flexible if you want to work from home. Many of the readers of this book will soon be working internationally on online freelancing platforms. You may get assignments from many countries, often at untypical times. Especially if you want to work in the customer support area, it can happen from time to time, when you work for international companies, that your working hours will not be the typical 9-5 job. It may be that you have to start working very early in some cases, sometimes very irregularly and in many situations even late into the night. You can assume that every working day will not be the same and that every day new tasks will come up to you.

5. Sales talent: As entrepreneurs or freelancers we are always dependent on getting new orders. However, it is usually not very easy to get clients, convince them of us and then get them to pay us. Having too few customers means financial ruin for us. Therefore it is important to have sales talent and to know how to use it.

   A good entrepreneur is a person who is able to build up reach and use it efficiently for his own purposes. Nothing else you have to do soon. So ask yourself if you are a person who can come out of your shell and have the talent to sell to someone else, or if you are the person who prefers not to approach other people. Of course you can also work from home as an introverted person, but it is very beneficial to be more extroverted.

6. Discipline: There will be many tasks that you simply do not want to do. Writing e-mails, bookkeeping, talking to customers, writing invoices and many other things will certainly not give you much pleasure. However, this is normal. You have to accept that not everything in your business will always be fun. There will be times when your business will not be good. But there will also be times when your business will have a big turnover. Even if times are tough, it is important to be disciplined and to work disciplined. The difference between a good and a bad entrepreneur is discipline. Set yourself daily goals and give everything to achieve them. Discipline is the easiest way to become successful. Because if you do every day what will move you forward, you will inevitably make progress and earn more money. Improve your discipline by not leaving your desk when you don't feel like it anymore, but only when you are done with your tasks.

7. Time: Many of us want to work from home because we believe that we will be able to take better care of our families and maybe even find the time to pursue our own hobbies. This is true to a certain extent, but many don't understand that especially in the beginning, when you start working from home, you are more likely to have less time than in your employment. This is due to the fact that in the beginning you have to build up your own financial infrastructure. Nobody gives you money and you have to make sure that the money

ends up in your account every month. And just this task turns out to be more difficult than you thought. That's exactly why you should really be sure that the idea you had before you started working at home really works and makes a profit. Also keep in mind that the initial period will also cause many problems. Therefore, it makes sense to take more time than you think you need at the beginning of your self-employment to build up income streams. In this way, you can take precautions and react more relaxed later if problems arise. Basically, you should also know how to manage your time. Just because you work from home does not mean that everyday tasks will disappear.

Most people find it difficult to find the balance between the two. There is the kind of person who tries to spend as much time as possible to make money, and there is also the kind of person who tries to work as little as possible. In both cases we are talking about extremes. A workload between the two extremes is probably more appropriate and purposeful. Managing one's own time means above all to value time and to know how important time really is. While many people look forward to their end of work, you will often work irregularly and your end of work will often not be a real end of work. To achieve your goals, you should try to make the most of your time and work as efficiently as possible. Discipline is again the key. The more disciplined you are in your work, the more breaks you can take.

8. Confidence: You need self-confidence to prevail over your doubts and other people's doubts. There will be many people who believe that you will fail. There will be some people who believe that you are simply not made to be an entrepreneur. And maybe self-doubt will come to you and you will think of yourself that you just don't have what it takes to be financially successful. Especially at the beginning of your entrepreneurial career you will be full of self-doubt. However, it is precisely these self-doubts that need to be overcome as quickly as possible. Because self-doubt will not get you anywhere, it will only hold you back. A healthy amount of doubt about your own work can be helpful, but self-doubt can also eat you up mentally and make you incapable of action. This must be prevented. Therefore, you should be able to see beyond your own doubts at the beginning and be able to trust yourself, even if not everything is going perfectly and you are possibly on the verge of failure. You should also be able to recognize when it makes sense to fail and not to continue. Throughout your life, look at your situation as objectively as possible. Sometimes it can make sense to give up and admit to yourself that you have failed. However, this should be the last resort. You should give everything before to not end up in this situation. If you should end up in this situation despite all your efforts, at least you know that there is nothing you could have done about your failure.

Many entrepreneurs have often been close to ruin and each time they managed to get out of this situation. Every failure only leads to you becoming mentally stronger and correcting your mistakes. The people who spend their whole life in an employment relationship will usually never have such experiences. And that's exactly why it can make sense not to give up directly, but to see failure as a lesson for your own life. And to hold on to this idea you need self-confidence.

Business registration, freelancer status or employment

Your first day, when you don't have to drive to work, but can work from home, will be an exciting one. However, before you can start working from home, you should also think about which professional situation is most suitable for you. Should you register a business, choose freelancer status or get a permanent job?

Employment

Choosing a job can make sense if you really want to play it safe and not take any risks. If you already have a job, it would be worth asking your boss if it would be possible to work from your home office. Many companies are already switching to working from home. In some companies it is even possible to work from home every day. Most other companies at least offer that employees can work from home on one or more days every week.

So ask your boss if such an option could be worthwhile for you and if your company already offers home-based work. If not, you have other alternatives to work from home, but you should be willing to quit your current job.

Such jobs are often referred to as remote jobs. You can, with a short search on the Internet, find exactly such jobs. Websites like the Indeed job platform allow you to search for remote jobs. Many positions are also simply referred to as "remote". Many of these companies that offer such jobs pay exactly the same as your previous employer. Many people are worried that they won't get paid much for their work as a remote jobber. This is not true in most cases.

Of course you should still check every offer carefully, because many companies that offer remote jobs have clear requirements. These are for example that you must have a university degree or that you have a fast internet connection. However, there are also many jobs for which you need almost no qualifications. These jobs are usually in the customer service or telecommunications sector. However, many companies also require you to visit the office at least once a week. You should check all these points with your future employer.

Many remote jobs can be easily found via the Internet. Many people see this as an opportunity to introduce themselves informally. But this is exactly what you should not do. Just because a company offers you a job online and you don't even have to come for an interview, doesn't mean you don't need a resume or a cover letter. You should try to be more professional than you already are, because the competition online is very competitive. You are probably not the only one who has applied for this job. There are certainly dozens of other applicants who have applied for this one job.

Many companies do not expect you to come for an interview, but there are some companies that would like to have a video chat interview with you. I think it goes without saying that you should not appear in a t-shirt and with unwashed hair for this interview. Dress as you would for a regular interview.

Before you sign an employment contract, you should read it carefully and see if you are actually employed by the company or if they only pay you for a freelance job. Many remote jobs are not permanent jobs, but rather one-time payments every month, which you have to pay tax on as a freelancer or through your business.

Also pay attention to who pays your social security contributions. Many companies do not do this in the remote job sector and it becomes your job to insure yourself.

Freelancer status

Registering for freelancer status has many advantages, but also some disadvantages. As a freelancer, you are no longer dependent on just one employer. You can and should do business with many different clients. By the way, you should not depend on only one employer, because this could easily be seen as a bogus self-employment by tax offices. It is always better to have many different customers or sources of income.

As a freelancer you have the opportunity to build many different online revenue streams at the same time. Now that you no longer have an employer, there is no one to tell you whether you can do other things besides work or build up other income streams. You also no longer have to worry about whether your employer has finally transferred your money to you and whether your pay slip is correct.

Now you also have the freedom to build up passive sources of income and serve customers from all over the world. You can sell not only services but also products worldwide and soon you will have enough customers to cover your monthly expenses. And do not forget: there are no limits to your income. If you work hard enough and make an effort every day, you will soon earn much more than you would in your regular employment.

But also remember that as a freelancer you have to take care of your own bookkeeping. You should hire a tax consultant, keep your receipts in order and possibly write invoices. For many, this task seems to be very complicated at first. In reality, accounting tasks can be reduced to a minimum by a tax consultant. Usually, one day a month is enough to sort your outgoing and incoming documents and file them. It is also recommended that you first take an accounting course before you choose freelancer status. This can prevent many problems.

Register a business

Registering a business is not that different from the freelancer status, especially if you register a sole proprietorship. Of course, I can only comment on German companies, but even internationally it is usually easy to distinguish between natural persons and legal entities.

For example, if you register a sole proprietorship, you are still liable without limitation because you and the sole proprietorship are the same person. This is also called a natural person. However, if you set up a limited company, you are only liable to a limited extent because the company is separate from you, the natural person. The company would then be called a legal entity.

Registering a business usually does not take very long in Germany. A sole proprietorship can usually be registered within 24 hours, if you don't count the registration at the tax office into the time. And many legal entities, such as a GmbH or a UG can be founded within 3 weeks to 8 weeks.

Of course you also have to do accounting for other business forms, but this process can also be streamlined by tax consultants.

Especially in their first year as entrepreneurs, many people are still very much afraid that their tax advisor will cost them a lot of money. However, in most cases this is not the case. If no high income is generated and few receipts are submitted, the annual expenses for the tax consultant usually remain in the three-digit range or small four-digit range. What is certain, however, is that it is usually less than most of us expect.

What would I recommend - employment, freelancer status or a business? I would recommend you to choose the freelancer status or to register a business. Why? Because with these two options you have much more options than in a pure employment. You will be surprised how easy it can be to make money online and above all to earn more than in an employment relationship. By getting hired, you are taking away many of the opportunities you would have had if you had chosen freelancer status or registered a company.

Most people are concerned about regularity and safety. That's why they choose to be employed. However, this is a fallacy. You are much safer when you are an entrepreneur. Why? Because you will build your own financial infrastructure. You control how you earn money. And once you have a customer base that keeps coming back to you, you will have regular income.

From my own experience I can also confirm that you will get a feeling for which business ideas are worthwhile at some point. You only have to rely on your own experience and start to implement your ideas.

How much money do you want to make?

One question that far too few people ask themselves is: How much money do I want to earn? Many of us do not need millions of Euros every year. Most people do not even need a hundred thousand Euros a year. Our aspirations may be great, but in reality we get by with much less.

Before you start making money from home, you should set yourself a realistic financial goal. Think about how much money you need to earn to cover all your running costs. Running costs can include insurance, rent for the apartment or house, food, clothing and perhaps money for restaurants and consumer goods. You will be surprised how many things you can do without and how few things you actually need in your life. Try to find out the absolute minimum in your calculations. Your calculation should not include unnecessary costs. Let's say you need 1500 Euros net each month to make ends meet. If you live frugally and have no children or partner, this should be a sum you can live on.

You have thus defined your first financial goal. Now you have to achieve this first goal. Later in this book we will take a closer look at the topic of goal setting, but already now I can tell you that your first financial goal is much easier to achieve than you think.

The more money you make, the more your mindset will change. In the beginning you just try to make ends meet to reach this minimum goal. But once you reach that goal, the world is open to you, you can experiment, develop and test new ideas, and live free from the pressure.

By the way, if you set up your business properly, you can work from anywhere in the world. This alone can often reduce your costs considerably. Most people assume that living away from home is much more expensive than living in your home country. However, this is a fallacy. Cheap prices in emerging markets and third world countries make it possible. Countries like Thailand or Indonesia already attract millions of visitors every year. Many of these visitors are digital nomads who can work from anywhere in the world. One of these people could also be you one day. Here in this book I will show you some of the sources of income that can make such a life possible. So build up your business with care and make sure that you don't build up sources of income that don't make you independent of location.

In the following we will now look at how to register a trade and thus lay the foundation for a successful entrepreneurial career.

CHAPTER 2: Developing a business idea and preparing a business plan

Developing a business idea

You should have your business idea completely thought through before you register your business. Although this may seem obvious, many people do not.

Many first-time entrepreneurs believe that their idea will work and that their product or service will find a buyer. Unfortunately, in reality this is not always the case. Therefore, you should test your idea before you focus all your attention on this one idea.

You should know that your idea works before you start to implement it. You may be wondering how exactly that's going to work. Just about every idea has been tried before. Check the Internet to see if there are other people who have tried the idea you want to implement. Or if you want to take a remote job, see what difficulties other people have had and what the expected monthly income is. The best thing is to contact these people personally and ask if it would be possible to talk. You will be surprised how many people will actually say "yes".

But how exactly does one develop a profitable business idea? You should think about the following points if you want to develop a profitable business idea

• Search for a problem and find a solution

- Competitor's offer

- Price and willingness to pay

- Marketing and sales

Many of your customers have a problem. For example, they want to lose weight, but don't know how. Or their heating doesn't work and they are looking for someone to look at their heating and repair it. Another person devotedly rides through the city every day, riding his bike through broken glass lying on the road. Currently he has to buy new tyres once a month. There are solutions for all these problems. People have looked closely, noticed what people need and then found a solution to people's problems. This is exactly why there are acceptance coaches or heating technicians or anti-flat tires for the bicycle. This is exactly what you have to do now. You have to develop a product or a service that helps people.

Whether you offer a product or a service, you should always remember that your product should be a solution to an existing problem. Only in very few cases is there no demand and yet the supply is accepted by the market.

In order to find a problem, you should first of all talk to other people, ask them about their problems and then record statistically how often this problem occurs. For example, if only one person in the whole world has a certain problem that no one else has, you can assume that solving the problem will not make the entrepreneur a lot of money. Because after one customer has solved his problem, there will be no one else who has this problem. Although this may sound exaggerated, it is a common occurrence in the pharmaceutical industry, namely when a single person has a previously unknown disease.

In practice, however, one can say that such problems occur very rarely. Nevertheless, you should make sure that your product or service has a clear purpose and solves a problem for many people, not just one person. To find this problem, you can do market research.

Market research is important in order to clearly identify what problems the customer is facing and to measure how big your potential competitors are.

To be able to do market research, you should first of all develop a list of questions. This questionnaire will later be presented to your potential customers. This questionnaire should consist of a maximum of thirty questions and should aim at the following points:

- Description of existing problems

- Description of the existing offer

- Marketing methods used by your competition to attract customers

- Willingness to pay of your customers

- Definition of the potential target group

Make sure that your questions are clear and aim to get accurate answers from your participants. When we ask questions for this purpose, we do not necessarily want short answers, but long clear answers that tell us exactly why a customer is dissatisfied with a competitor's product or service or why the price-performance ratio is not right. Short answers usually do not help us in this respect.

In the following we will take a closer look at the above points and find out how best to ask questions for our purposes.

- Description of existing problems: Your goal is to find out what problems your potential customers have with the competitor's product or service. Does the product not work as the customer expects it to? Is the product no longer up to date? Is it too expensive or does it not have essential functions? These are the topics you should talk about with your potential customers. For example, ask the following questions:

  1. What problems do you encounter with the current use of the product?

  2. Which functions of the product are essential for you and why?

  3. Which functions could you do without and why?

  4 Which functions would you like to have and why? Would these justify a higher price point?

  Always make sure that your questions do not lead to short unclear answers. If a question invites short answers, add "...and why?" to the question.

- Description of the existing offer: Now it should be a matter of talking openly with the customer about the competitor's range of services and asking what the customer expects from the product. For example, you could ask your customer the following questions:

  1. What made you accept the offer from the company (your competitor)?

  2. If you could define a function that is particularly important to you, what would it be and why?

  3. How would you describe it?

  4. What is the unique selling point of the company's offer?

  5. What was your first impression of the company's product?

  6 What negative things did you notice about the company's offer?

- Marketing methods: Analyzing your competitor's marketing methods is crucial for your business success. Through your surveys you can find out what your competitor has already tried and which strategies have worked and which strategies have not worked. Here are some questions you could ask your potential customer:

  1. Where did you first learn about the company's product?

  2. Through which other channels did you come across the product or the company behind the product?

  3. How was the company's advertising structured? Which sales argument was in the foreground?

4. Optional: Where were the company's products positioned in the store?

- Customers' willingness to pay: What price are your potential customers willing to pay for your product or service? Is this price below the price you calculated, above it or maybe even exactly where you imagined it? You will find answers to all these questions. Especially the pricing and the price-performance ratio are crucial in a competitive market and whoever provides the best quality and the best offer will win in the end. You could ask the following questions to your potential customer to find out more about his willingness to pay:
1. How much money did you spend on the product? Would you do it again and if so, why?
2. What price point do you think is appropriate for this product and why?
3. How would you rate the price-performance ratio?

- Definition of the potential target group: After you have interviewed all participants, you should also roughly write down what characteristics the participants had. Try to find commonalities and write down what common motives your potential customers had. The following factors could be useful for you to define your target group: Gender of potential customers, age, location, interests, political views, educational background, fears and more.

By the end of the analysis you will have found commonalities that will allow you to look for more people with the same commonalities in the future. You know that these people are most likely to buy from you in the future.

Writing a business plan

If you have decided to register a company or choose freelancer status, you should write a business plan for your work. It is useful to write a business plan to have in writing what you want to do and what you don't want to do, what the risks of the business are, what the running costs will be and what could all go wrong. A business plan can also be useful if you need financial support from banks. Especially when money is in short supply, it can be worthwhile taking out a loan to finance the first few months of independence. Write your business plan while you are still in your employment, because once you have left it, you should only focus on your self-employment.

In the following we will now look at how to write a business plan. Your business plan should contain the following points:

1. Summary of your business: At the beginning of your business plan you should first define exactly what your business does, who you are, what your goal is and how your business is organized. In any case, keep it short. You should not write more than ten sentences on this point. This point is important for other people to quickly understand your

business. If you write the business plan only for yourself, you do not need to fill in this point.

2. Describe your business idea in detail: What exactly is your business idea? Describe your business idea clearly and concisely. What will you do or what steps have you taken so far? Where does the product stand and what functions does it currently have? Try to describe each individual business area and field of activity as precisely as possible. However, this does not include the organizational structure, but only the work that is done by your company. For example, suppose you want to open a shoe factory. At this point in the business plan, you could define what shoes you already produce, what shape they have, what types of shoes they are and what the unique selling point of the shoes is. At this point you can also start writing about the price and define which price point you consider appropriate.

It is also important that you list the individual functions. At a shoe manufacturer this could be that the shoes are made of leather, if you make sports shoes, you go into the suspension of the shoe and so on.

If you want to sell a service, at this point you should define the exact amount of work required. What exactly do you offer your customer? When is there a surcharge? How do services fit together? For example, are there services that you offer as an upsell or downsell for an existing service? At this point you can perform a so-called SWOT analysis.

SWOT stands for "strengths, weaknesses, opportunities, threats". To be able to do a SWOT analysis, you should first of all analyse what strengths your company has. What are you particularly good at? What is especially important about your service? How do these strengths express themselves? You should then show the weaknesses of your company. What are your current weaknesses? Where is there still room for improvement and which problems can you possibly not solve at the moment?

Once you are done with this, you should go into more detail about the opportunities that your company has or could have in the future. At this point, you can already go into market analysis and outline what overriding trends are in the market and what opportunities will arise for you and your company. Finally, you should also address threats to your business. Are there any trends or situations that could ruin your business? What problems could arise and what threats do these problems pose to your company?

Write a little too much for this point rather than a little too little, even if you never show the business plan to anyone else. The business plan should above all help you to develop your business.

3. Market and competitors: Who are your competitors and how successful are these competitors? How much market share does each major competitor have and is there still room for another company? It is important that you remain

completely objective at this point in your business plan. Many founders try to gloss over the market situation, as they hope to gain an advantage with potential investors. However, this is a fallacy. Many first-time founders also simply gloss over the market environment to make themselves feel better.

4. Marketing and Sales: At this point, you should discuss how you will sell your product to the customer. Would it be possible to sell the product via social media like Facebook, Instagram, Snapchat or LinkedIn or does it make more sense to spend money on newspaper advertising or TV commercials?

Before you make these considerations, you should already have looked at your competitors' marketing and sales strategies. Because only if you know what works and what doesn't work, you can make effective marketing and sales plans for your company.

If you ever present your business plan to lenders or investors, they will most likely want an estimate of how sales will be distributed across these different marketing and sales strategies. So ask yourself: Where will you generate the most sales? Which marketing method will be most efficient? And which methods will continue to generate profits in the future? Because not only your potential financiers, but also you, should not only be interested in how you will make your business profitable now, but rather how you will ensure that your business will be profitable over time.

Also, develop a practical plan for how you will sell your products to your customers and show alternatives in case a marketing strategy does not work.

5. Organization and your position: At this point you should now define who will work in your company. Explain which positions are to be filled. For example, do you need a secretary, do you need a marketing manager, managing director or do you need to fill other positions? If you are a one-man company, you should describe your position exactly and explain where your personal strengths lie.

6. Financing: How will your company be financed? Do you need financial help and if so, how much financial help do you need? If you need financial help, you should fan out what the investors' money will be spent on. What will you spend how much money on? Why is this expenditure necessary and, above all, will this expenditure bring money to the company? Potential expenses could be for example office costs, staff costs, insurance, material, marketing costs and many other things.

Always make sure that there are no spelling mistakes in your business plan. Your business plan is your figurehead and should be proofread by you several times. You should not only proofread the grammar and spelling, but also the logic and comprehensibility of the business plan. Is everything in the business plan really understandable? Can there be no misunderstandings? Is your position in the company clearly defined? Really try not to leave any question open. Even if you do not present your business plan to anyone else, it can be good for yourself and your documentation.

Implementing a business idea

What steps do you have to take to implement your business idea? You should start by going to your accountant and discussing the idea with him. Often first-time entrepreneurs are not aware of the different tax issues that go hand in hand with certain sources of income. It is important that you explain to your tax advisor openly and unembellished what exactly you want to do and which sources of income you plan to build up. For example, if you want to sell courses online, your tax advisor may ask you how the sale of these courses. Especially if you sell abroad, you may well owe VAT to other countries. Your tax advisor will point out possible problems and explain what you should and should not do. For example, if you sell courses online, the accountant will look into the contracts between you and the platform you are selling through. The accountant will look at who the contract is between, who is billing, who pays sales tax and so on. Exactly for this reason I suggest that first-time entrepreneurs look for a tax consultant. Such talks can save you a lot of trouble. My suggestion to you in general is therefore that you send a message to your tax consultant before you start a new income stream. Send any contracts, terms and conditions and the like to your tax consultant for inspection. Even if this might cost a few hundred Euros in the worst case, this is usually very helpful and will let you sleep better later because you don't have to worry about taxes.

After you have shown the sources of income to your accountant and he has approved them, you should start to define goals for yourself personally. These goals can be monetary or activity-based. I suggest you set two types of goals, short term goals and long term goals. A short term goal is a goal you can achieve in less than three months, a long term goal is a goal you will achieve in more than three months. First of all, define your long-term goal. This should be a really big goal. Suppose you would like to sell books through Amazon Kindle Publishing. Your goal is to have two hundred books published one day. At first glance, this goal seems astronomical, but that's exactly what our goal is. Then we'll think about what we need to do to reach that astronomical goal. Let us say that we want to reach this goal in five years. So we would have to write two hundred books in 1825 days. This means that we have to publish a new book every nine days or so. But the average Kindle books are usually only eighteen thousand words long. This would mean that we would have to write two thousand words every day. Most people manage to write up to four hundred words per ten minutes. To reach your goal, you would only need to write for fifty minutes every day. You should now go through the same thought process for your goal. Try to turn the big goal into many small goals. These are then your short-term goals. You only have to reach these small goals to reach your big goal one day. So you can reach big goals very easily. You just have to work continuously. That's all you have to do.

After you have defined your goals, I would develop a problem plan. Think about what can go wrong and how you will overcome these situations. Suppose you want to write books, but your books don't sell. What do you do then? At this point, you could look for another business activity as Plan B or target a remote job.

It is always good to have a realistic plan B. Spend as much time developing your Plan B as you do developing your Plan A. But make both plans before you start your own business. During the self-employment you should not think about your plan B, but really concentrate on plan A and do your best to put it into action.

After you have developed a problem plan, you should also develop a success plan. This could consist of new income streams or investments. Because when you earn your first money, you should already be thinking about how you can multiply it. If you diversified your money on the stock market, you would have created another income stream. You could also invest the money in your business and hire people to do the work for you, so you can focus on scaling up. Be one step ahead of yourself and keep thinking about how you can make your business grow even faster.

CHAPTER 3: 10 ways to make money from home

Virtual assistants jobs

Many successful companies are looking online for so-called virtual assistants. Virtual assistants help the entrepreneur to take over tasks for which the entrepreneur simply has no time left. These can be accounting tasks or answering e-mails or telephone calls, for example. A virtual assistant job can be versatile. Maybe you too will soon be making appointments for someone else, writing invoices, issuing reminders, solving problems or working on new ideas.

As a virtual assistant you will work completely remotely from home. You won't have to go to an office, otherwise you can do all your work from your computer.

As a virtual assistant you should always be ready to stand in for your employer. Many employers expect you to be spontaneous and quick to get things done for the employer.

Jobs as a virtual assistant can be found on freelancing platforms like Upwork, Fiverr or the platform Freelancer. To earn money as a freelancer, you should first of all create accounts on these different platforms. Upwork is in my opinion the most promising platform for virtual assistant jobs at the moment. When you sign up, you need to create a profile description and add a profile picture. Your profile picture should show you. It is recommended to have a profile picture where you can be seen well and where no other person is present. Please do not upload profile pictures that show you in a bad light. The client is looking for a professional person he can trust. Therefore, show yourself up close, smile on the picture and be professionally dressed. A nice shirt on the photo is usually enough to make a professional impression.

You should also include the following points in your profile description:

• Heading: Summarize in one sentence what you offer and why a client should choose you. This sentence is at the top of your description. This will be the first sentence your potential clients will read about you. And as we know, the first impression counts. So be on your best behavior and try to make a good first impression on the potential client.

• Field of activity: Next you should go into your field of activity. What exactly do you offer? Creating invoices and completing accounting tasks, writing business letters, taking over personal tasks, writing reports or something else? Define clearly what services you offer, but leave a little room for more. Your client wants you to provide individually tailored services. Therefore, it makes sense not to define the given services too much, but to give the potential employer the chance to think of own services for you.

When you specify the field of activity, try to set priorities and indicate what your strengths are. But also try to list as many fields of activity as possible. Each additional field of activity that you list could lead to another assignment. At this point you can also indicate that you are not only interested in short-time work, but that you are also willing to work with a person for a longer period of time.

- Experience: At this point you should now explain what experience you have gained so far. You could, for example, refer to work from your employment relationship. Let's assume, for example, that you have previously worked as a receptionist. You could write that this job required certain qualifications, skills and talents and that you gained new skills and knowledge through this job.

  If you wish, you can also simply list your complete CV or provide a link to it to your potential employer. You can also list higher degrees, if you have any. For example, if you have completed an apprenticeship, you could list it here in your profile. The same applies to university and college degrees. This is the kind of degree that could greatly increase your chances of getting a job.

  If you are already working online and would like to become a virtual assistant, I would suggest that you outline what you have been doing over the last few years and what skills were needed to perform your daily tasks.

- Sample work: A unique selling point could be your work. If you offer your services as a virtual assistant on platforms like Fiverr or Upwork, you should be able to show sample work. These examples could be a text that you have written, reports you have produced or successes you have achieved for your clients. It is better to offer too many examples than too few examples. Your clients will appreciate that you disclose your work. Of course you should only show your best work to your potential clients to increase your chances of getting a contract from them. Also, make sure that your samples fit the services you have listed and are prepared in an attractive format.

• The next step: Offer your potential clients a first free appointment where you both can get to know each other. This first free appointment can be done via video chat, for example. During this first appointment you explain to your potential client why he should choose you by showing him how you can help him.

Try to increase your chances of being discovered by clients by having a professionally designed profile. This will include pictures of you, maybe even one or more videos of you introducing yourself and your services and a description that will convince the potential client that you will add value to their business.

Create accounts on as many platforms as possible. You may not generate one new order per month on some platforms, but there will be some platforms where you will earn a lot of money. You will also very soon realize that multiple income streams can be worthwhile. Especially with online companies it happens again and again that certain income streams simply break away because platforms are no longer profitable, the algorithm of the platforms puts you at a disadvantage and so on. But also assume that you will fight for orders on all online platforms with many other virtual assistants. Therefore, you may sometimes sell below your value. Especially in the beginning, when no clients have given you ratings and nobody knows you, it can be useful to take many smaller orders to collect many good ratings and reviews.

However, before you offer your services on all these different platforms, you should talk to your tax advisor first. It is possible that certain platforms are disadvantageous for you from a tax point of view, that some don't care about the billing and maybe simply do something wrong that could harm you. A tax consultant usually has an eye for such problems and will point them out to you.

Tutor jobs

All over the world there are children and young people who need help at school or university. Some children just want to learn a language, others need help with their maths homework and still other children are just looking for someone to learn with. Tutor jobs are very fulfilling and usually well paid jobs that you can do from home.

Some of you will certainly be thinking now and wondering what skills you have that you can pass on to you in the form of lessons.

If you know German, you can already earn money as a tutor. There are many platforms that are desperately looking for people who can speak German. Students want to learn German and talk to a German, to hear the language from the mouth of a native speaker or simply to improve their own language skills.

If you speak English, you can teach English to students all over the world. Especially the Chinese market is very interesting for such activities. Platforms like VIPKids, QKids or Landi English allow you to teach students from China online from your computer. Many of the students from China are very eager to learn and are looking forward to the appointment with you. In most cases you will not be teaching classes, but only individuals. This creates a very private and relaxed atmosphere. For example, you teach the child for an hour, you go through some exercises together, solve them together and check possible homework. The lessons take place via video chat. So the child can see you and you can see the child. It is advisable to bring a whiteboard and some pens so that you can show the child from your side how certain things work. Many platforms want you to give the child homework. This homework is then checked by you, usually in your personal free time, and then evaluated in a lesson with the child.

If you don't want to teach English, but are more familiar with topics such as mathematics, biology, computer science, art, social sciences, literature or something else, then platforms like Chegg are worthwhile. Chegg is also an online tutor platform where you can offer your services as a tutor. Chegg is also very similar in the way it works. With Chegg all lessons are done via video chat and the students get homework from you.

Many online tutoring platforms take a small commission for every hour sold through the platform. However, many platforms also simply give you orders and you don't know for how much money the platform has sold the lesson with you to the student. And then there are some other platforms that pay you a fixed amount per hour.

But how much money can one earn on such platforms? Platforms like Chegg are more known for paying little money per hour. Many Chinese platforms pay well. In most cases tutors earn between 6 Euro and 25 Euro per hour online. Before you start working on online tutor platforms, it is recommended to talk to tutors who already work on these platforms. They will be able to tell you better about the work you will have to do if you want to teach on the specific platform.

But remember: The great advantage of online tutor jobs is that you can take them from all over the world. You don't have to be at a fixed location, you can travel around the world and just need a good internet connection to be able to do the lessons. And it may very well be that you will not have a particularly high cost in the country you are travelling to. So if you work on a platform where you get a good hourly wage, you may only have to work three or four hours a day to cover all expenses.

The activity of the online tutor can also be very fulfilling for many. While many activities that can be done from home are mostly mindless, tutor jobs are much more interesting. You will really grow fond of some of the students and maybe even make personal connections with parents worldwide. A lot can come out of such relationships. Above all, the gratitude of the children will give the job a meaning and motivate you to continue teaching the children.

Is tutor work something for you now? Yes and no. Yes, you should become a tutor if you have a passion for teaching other people and helping them with problems. And no, you shouldn't become a tutor if it's just about making money and you don't want to build a relationship with your students.

Freelancing activities

There are practically endless ways to earn money as a freelancer. You could offer designs, work as a virtual assistant, develop websites, help with marketing and much more. But before you start working as a freelancer, you should ask yourself the following questions:

- Can I market myself and convince other people of me and my services?

- Am I willing to work on tasks with which I do not feel one hundred percent comfortable?

- Am I flexible and can I adapt to my environment?

- Can I be relied upon and do I carry out tasks with the utmost care?

- Don't I ever give up and get up again when I fail?

- Do I treat other people with respect and know how to behave towards customers?

- Am I willing to take responsibility and stick to agreements?

After you have asked and answered these questions, you should think of a precise niche for your activity. You should offer something that is currently in demand and where there is not much supply. Such niches are very difficult to find. Above all, look for niches in which you can earn money. No one can do everything. Neither can you. Which is exactly why you should only offer services that you can actually perform. Listen to yourself and try to understand what you are really good at and what you are not. Being honest with yourself is the first step to financial success. People who are not honest with themselves and offer services that nobody needs will quickly disappear from the scene. Next, you should define your offer.

- Service description: Define for yourself which services you would like to offer as a freelancer. In order to be able to define the amount of work, you should first ask yourself what you are particularly good at. Write these things down and arrange them in groups. Then think about which services could be particularly profitable. If you are unsure about this, a search on freelancing platforms like Upwork might help. Take a look at how much money the freelancers in this niche have already earned and exchange ideas with them to find out more about the niche.

Then you should define how long you need for a certain service. Let's assume you create logos for other people. How long does it take you to create this logo? Is it worth it for you? Or do you spend too much time making little money? Your service effort consists of two key figures: the time you need to complete a service and a definition of what the service is exactly about. Next, we want to determine the price for the service.

- Pricing: Think of an hourly wage that you would really like to earn one day. Let's say your goal is to earn a hundred Euros per hour. Now you have to ask yourself how you want to achieve this goal. One way would be to offer a service that allows such an hourly wage. Let's say, for example, that you take two hundred Euros for a professional logo. To create this logo, you need four hours. This would reduce your hourly wage to just fifty Euros. So now you have to think about how you can improve your hourly wage. This could be done by offering additional services, such as creating a 3D mockup or making the source file available to the client. By offering these extra services, which cost you almost no time, you can increase your income per customer and therefore your hourly rate. Another strategy to increase the hourly rate is to simply let other people do the work. You could hire a person in a third country who wants a much lower hourly wage for the same work. Especially in Eastern Europe and Southeast Asia there are many freelancers who could do such work for you for cheap money. For example, you could pay this freelancer twenty euros per hour. This freelancer manages to do the work in four hours like you and would like to get eighty Euros from you. Your profit on this job is one hundred and twenty euros, even though you have not actually done any work actively.

- Personal minimum price: However, there will be times when you cannot always charge a high hourly wage. If the cash registers are empty at times, you should also take orders that are not optimal. In this way you can prevent the possible insolvency of your company and ensure that money continues to be collected from you. However, you should also define a minimum price for yourself. The minimum price means a minimum hourly wage. Ask yourself: What is the minimum hourly rate I would work for in bad times?

- Price-performance ratio: Is the price-performance ratio right for your customer? Your customer expects high quality results from you. Especially if a customer pays you a lot of money, he will be very careful to get only the best quality. Compare your price-performance ratio with the price-performance ratio of your competitors. Is your price-performance ratio better or rather worse?

- Upsells/Downsells: After a customer has bought services from you, he should receive another offer from you. A downsell is typically a product or service that is sold to you after you have already purchased a product or service. In our case, this service should be cheaper than the first service the customer bought from us. Upsells, on the other hand, are services that are more expensive than the first service a customer bought from us. Why should one offer upsells or downsells? Upsells and downsells help to increase the revenue per customer. This is especially useful if you invest time and money in customer acquisition. Let's assume, for example, that you place advertisements on the Internet. You spend a thousand Euros on advertising and through these thousand Euros you get ten customers who buy from you. Each customer pays you on average seventy euros. So with these ten customers you have earned seven hundred Euros. At first glance, it seems as if you have made a loss. But this is a fallacy. Through upsells and downsells you can increase your income considerably and make a profit. So upsells and downsells help you to generate profits faster.

- Price of extra activities: Are there any extras you'd like to offer? Are there volume discounts or associated services? You should define all these things before you decide to work as a freelancer.

Transcriptions

With transcriptions it is very easy to make money if you know how. What exactly is a transcription? A transcription is the exact transcription of a text to the letter and word. These transcriptions can be made from audio and video files.

There are many fields of activity in the field of transcriptions. You can work on online job platforms, you can work on specialized freelancing platforms or you can build your own agency.

In order to be able to make transcriptions, you should speak the language in which you are to make transcriptions perfectly. Making transcriptions is not as easy as you think. Often you will get jobs where the audio recording you are transcribing is particularly bad. In such cases, you will often guess more than you actually understand what the speaker is saying in the audio recording.

You should also be able to type fast. Creating transcriptions can take some time. The faster you can type, the better. If you get an audio or video recording of the speaker speaking slowly, you might even be able to transcribe the entire speech as the person speaks. However, most of you will not be able to do this at first. This usually requires a lot of practice. And especially when the speakers speak very fast, it is almost impossible to make a transcription directly while listening.

A very easy way to earn money with transcriptions is to accept jobs through the GoTranscript platform. There you can take orders at any time and work them off. Most of the time, you will receive one US dollar for one minute of audio recording that you convert into a transcription. If you can convert forty minutes of audio per day into transcriptions, for example, you could earn forty dollars a day through this platform.

Of course, there are also alternatives such as the TranscribeMe or Rev. Both platforms offer the possibility of taking orders directly and processing them.

Of course you can still offer this service as a freelancer via platforms like Upwork or Fiverr. There is always a need for freelancers on these platforms who can do transcriptions. Usually you earn a little more on Fiverr or Upwork than on platforms like GoTranscript or TranscribeMe.

If you are fluent in several languages, I would also recommend that you offer your transcriptions in these languages. Usually you can offer transcriptions for other languages besides English for more money per minute. You should generally take care not to sell your work for less than its value. Unfortunately there is a lot of competition among freelancers in the transcription business online. Stand up to these competitors by staying true to your line. You don't have to undercut other people, but convince through quality.

In the transcription field, too, it is important not only to build up one source of income, but to have many different sources of income. For example, you could offer your services on GoTranscript, TranscribeMe, Rev, Fiverr, Upwork, People Per Hour and many other platforms. You can also use your services to reach people who need help and are not looking for freelancers through online platforms. Keep an eye out for local companies or even internationally operating companies that might need help in this area.

Sell online courses

One of the easiest ways to make money online is to sell online courses. Online courses usually consist of video material, exercise sheets, quizzes and personal help. An online lecturer who sells courses over the Internet can build up a passive income through his or her work. It would be possible to sell courses through online platforms such as Udemy or Skillshare, but you can also sell courses through your own website or through a reseller.

Why should you create courses online at all? Creating a course is not very complicated. All you need is a camera or webcam, a good microphone and editing software. If you want, you can also buy a green screen and softboxes to light up the recording area. But that's all you need. With online courses you can currently still make a quick profit. Online courses are available in every price range. There are courses that are offered for a few Euros and other courses that are offered for thousands of Euros. Online courses allow you to build many other sources of income. For example, you could take your online courses and publish them on many online platforms. Udemy and Skillshare are among the largest online course platforms, but there are many more. You could publish your courses on at least ten platforms and earn money on each of them. You would have created ten new revenue streams. You can also take your videos from the online courses and post some of them on YouTube for free. Once your channel has a thousand subscribers and the necessary watchtime for the videos has been reached, you can monetize these videos and have built up another source of income. You can continue to offer your courses on your own online course platform. Such course platforms can be built with little effort and little money. Software like Teachable can help you to build a fully functional online course platform within a few hours. You can then start monthly memberships on this platform and thus build up a passive income. And if that wasn't enough, you can also convert your videos into books. On YouTube you can download the transcript for each of your videos. Then you can hire a freelancer on platforms like Fiverr or Upwork to make a book for you from the transcriptions. You can then sell them again on platforms like Amazon Kindle and build another passive income stream.

However, you should also go into the field of online courses, because it will continue to be a promising niche in the future. People always want to learn something new and you can help them to understand these new things.

If you want to create an online course, you should first of all consider what your strengths are. What exactly can you do? What would people pay money for? Which topics are currently in high demand? You should write down your ideas and start generating the first course idea. Once you have found a topic, you should start developing a table of contents for the course. Start by writing down the main points. You should now build your course around these main points.

To develop a more precise structure, you should also look at how other lecturers teach their online courses. How are the courses structured? What is the focus of these lecturers and are there things you can do better? Take notes and then develop your table of contents in a text document. This does not have to be the final table of contents. Many of the points will only become apparent to you when you start recording the course. So don't be too much of a perfectionist. In the process of recording, you will come up with many new ideas and it would be a shame to have to ignore them.

Once you have finished your table of contents, you should start preparing your content. Think about how you would like to record videos. Do you want to be seen in the video and how do you want to convey the knowledge? Many students like to see the teacher during the video. However, if you don't want to show yourself, this is not a disaster.

I would also recommend that you record one video after another. Many teachers prepare the whole course first and then start shooting the videos. I find it more useful to prepare a video, then record it, prepare another one and then record the next video again. Why? Because it helps you to stay motivated. A lot of people take a long time to prepare all the content and get frustrated. Many people then completely stop with online courses. However, when you prepare a video and record it right away, you feel like you've completed something and taken a step forward.

If you can motivate yourself well and are disciplined, you can prepare the whole course first and only then take it. If you don't have these qualities, I would suggest that you complete one video after another.

The next step is to publish your course and find first customers. There are many ways to do this. For one thing, you can publish your courses on platforms like Udemy or Skillshare. These offer you organic reach. So you don't have to advertise or focus on marketing your course to generate sales. These platforms usually take a commission for each sale. Commissions range from zero percent to more than eighty percent in some cases. However, you can also sell your courses through so-called resellers. Resellers are platforms that buy your course from you and resell it to an end customer. This method usually also makes the tax situation easier for you. These resellers take a small commission for each sale. This commission is usually between zero and ten percent. If you do not want to publish on online platforms and you do not want to use resellers, you can sell your products on your own website. In this case you are responsible for billing, accounting and paying any taxes.

Build and scale an agency

To build up an agency is the current trend. Especially on social media there seem to be new people every day who want to encourage you to start your own agency. But what is actually behind this excitement? An agency is not much more than a company that offers services to its end customers. As we have already found out, there are practically infinite services that one could offer. Especially marketing agencies are in high demand at the moment. However, design, IT and ghostwriting agencies also seem to sprout up every day. So building up an agency doesn't mean much more than simply offering services.

You start an agency by thinking about which services you want to offer. Let's assume you would like to offer marketing services, then you should think about which marketing services are currently in high demand. Get in touch with other agencies and try to exchange ideas with them.

The following niches are currently in great demand:

- **Marketing agencies:** A marketing agency can offer a variety of services. Your customer is usually looking for ways to generate more customers or sell his products. Especially the online area seems to be new territory for many companies. Exactly for this reason these companies need support in finding customers online. You could help them by placing advertisements, setting up a content marketing strategy, helping them to find mistakes or restructuring their marketing. What many companies are looking for is a competent partner. The cost is not a big issue for many companies, because they assume that you will help them. Companies expect you to bring about rapid change. Therefore it is important that you are familiar with what you are offering. There are too many agencies that give bad advice and do not produce profitable results. So your goal should be to show your competence and convince your client of your services.

It should not be too difficult for you to get customers. After all, you have a marketing agency. You could call local companies and ask them if they need help with their marketing. Or you could place ads yourself and try to get people to sign up for a free initial call with you. Finally, you could set up a YouTube channel and demonstrate your skills in videos. By proving what you can do, you'll make a good first impression and get people to contact you.

- **Ghostwriting agencies:** Another way to make money from home with an agency is to offer ghostwriting services. Ghostwriting means that you write a book for someone else and they can use the book for their own purposes without having to name you as the author. This field of activity has become very profitable in the recent past as more and more entrepreneurs need e-books for their website or online shop and more and more people want to build up passive income through Amazon Kindle. For such types of business models like Amazon Kindle, the entrepreneur needs many books. Let's assume that you can turn over a small book for five hundred Euros and an entrepreneur orders fifty books from you, then you earn 25000 Euros with one client alone. In very rare cases this is the case with other types of agencies. In ghostwriting these figures are typical. So it may well be that you only need a handful of profitable clients to earn six figures a year. Start a YouTube channel, show how to make money with Amazon Kindle on that YouTube channel, and then say in your videos that you offer ghostwriting services. As soon as you get some reach, the first people will start asking you about it and want to order books from you. The key is to get customers to buy from you again and again. This can be done by contacting the customer repeatedly and asking them if they want more books, or you can make a big deal from the start for ten books for example.

You can bill for your services yourself or you can offer your services via platforms such as Fiverr. However, it is best to offer not only ghostwriting via freelancing platforms, but also translation. For example, you could translate the e-books you have already written for other people into other languages. This could greatly increase your revenue per client.

- **IT agencies:** Many companies need websites. You could help with an IT agency. The easiest way to get to companies that need a website is to go to the Yellow Pages website. Thousands of local companies are listed there. Many of these companies don't have a website listed, or only have a website listed that is not very representative. My tip to you at this point would be to find these companies and record them in a table. Then you should call these companies and tell them about your services. You could, for example, offer these entrepreneurs that you take care that the company gets a professional website for small money. If you call the companies, I would not make my offer immediately, but rather describe what you do and ask for a personal meeting. Offer something free of charge to get your foot in the door of the customer. You could offer to create a design draft for the customer's website. The customer can then decide whether he wants to have the website or not. And, at the same time, you should also give the customer a reason to buy from you by saying that you provide a best price guarantee. The customer should know that he will always get the best price from you.

Once the website is up and running, you should start upselling and downselling. For example, you could offer to take care of the site and write a new blog article every week, or you could offer to take care of the SEO technical optimization of the website and so on. All these services can be charged separately as upsell or downsell. This way you increase the profitability per client.

Of course, you can not only offer website development, you could also go into game development, apps, digitalization, general consulting and many other areas.

- **Design agencies:** Every business needs a logo, possibly social media banners, promotional materials like flyers, video editing and much more. And this will most likely not change in the near future. Opening an agency in the design field could be a wise decision, because designs are always needed. Your potential clients are most likely companies. These companies expect creative excellence and a reasonable price-performance ratio from you. Successful design agencies live on their example work. When you start a design agency, make sure that your website contains a portfolio. This portfolio will be the figurehead for your company. Therefore, list only your best designs in this portfolio. The portfolio should of course also match your workload. For each service that is part of your effort, there should be a sample work that the potential customer can look at. Clients for a design agency can be found in many different ways. However, cold email and social media marketing work best.
However, not only companies need designs, but often also freelancers and individuals. Business models like the T-shirt business need many professional designs. Exactly for such business models you could provide a contact point with your agency. You could offer t-shirt designs and help people build a t-shirt business with exciting t-shirt design ideas.

Once you have written down the niche of your service, you should register your business. You do not necessarily have to start your agency on your own. You can also set up the agency in cooperation with someone else.

Before you go to the office and register your agency, you should think about the legal form of the company. By the way, in most cases you don't need an office for your agency and can do all your work from home. If you have a personal meeting with a company, you can offer to drive to the company or meet in a restaurant.

All in all, it can be said that the agency model is more attractive than ever. Many entrepreneurs are looking for professional service providers and are willing to pay good money for a service. All you have to do now is make a decision and start to win the first customers.

Sell designs

As a designer you can earn money in many ways. You can offer your services on online freelancing platforms, start your own agency, but you also have the possibility to offer online courses on design, write books on the subject, sell on marketplace platforms, build a t-shirt or icon business and much more. As a designer you have almost endless possibilities to make money online.

T-shirt business

A t-shirt business is a very easy way to make money with designs. Many people buy t-shirts for different purposes online. Some people are going to have a bachelor party and need t-shirts for it, others need t-shirts for their sports team and still others just want to buy a t-shirt with a funny saying on it.

Many people buy their t-shirts on online marketplace platforms like Merch by Amazon or Spreadshirt. On these platforms you can earn money by uploading t-shirt designs to the respective platforms. The concept is actually quite simple. You upload your designs and the platforms take care of printing your designs on the t-shirts as soon as the platform receives an order. The platform will also send the t-shirts for you and take care of the billing. The only thing you have to do is to create t-shirt designs. Even if you can't design, you can still make money with this business model. You just have to find someone who will create the designs for you. On platforms like Upwork or Fiverr you will find many talented designers who can create designs for you for little money. Try to hire just one designer for your project through these platforms. You only need one reliable designer to start with, one who doesn't steal designs from the internet, but creates your own designs. You can also find such designers for even less money on platforms in countries where most people don't make much money. One example is the Philippine platform onlinejobs.ph.

If you decide to search for designers on these platforms, you should pay attention to the following things:

- Price per design: You should never spend more than ten Euros per design. We want to become profitable as quickly as possible, so it doesn't make sense if the individual designs are too expensive.
- Quality: The designs that your designer creates for you should be of high quality. Bad designs will not sell and generate more costs than revenue. If you would not buy your own t-shirt designs, you should not try to sell them to other people.
- Originality: Your designer should have created all designs himself. Do not try to take designs from the Internet. Tell your designer to send you the preparation for each design. This way you can be sure that the designer really draws each design himself.

Afterwards you only have to scale. Try to create designs for different niches and upload them to marketplace platforms. Over time, visitors to the marketplace platforms will notice you and buy from you.

Icon business

An icon business is very similar to a t-shirt business. You create icons or have icons created and publish them on icon marketplace platforms. In my opinion the most promising marketplace platform is thenounproject and also the platform Iconfinder. On these platforms you can upload your icon designs. You just have to name them and tag them and wait for the first ones to sell.

You can have icons created by freelancers on platforms like Fiverr and Upwork. However, you should not spend more than three Euros per icon. After all, we don't want to wait years for our first profits, but maybe just a few months.

Make sure that you publish a variety of different icons. Especially popular styles are the glyph, 2D and outline style. These types of icons sell particularly well on marketplace platforms.

Even an icon business has to be skilfully scaled. Develop icons for many different niches and upload them to the different platforms. Over time, the first revenues will arrive.

Freelancing in the design area

Design services can be sold very well via online freelancing platforms. People per Hour or also Upwork are common platforms to work as freelancers. While many designers try to offer their designs at the lowest possible prices, it could also be your unique selling point to offer high quality designs for a little more money. It is also important in this business that you not only build up one income stream, but many. Try to work on several freelancing platforms, sell services through your own website and maybe offer related products like online courses, books or other information material.

Marketplace design platforms

Platforms like Creative Market and Envato Elements allow designers to make money online with their designs. You can offer a wide variety of designs on these platforms. For example, you could offer Powerpoint designs or Keynote presentations, icons, stock photography, videos, 3D templates, website templates and much more.

This type of platform also works according to the marketplace principle. You create the designs, upload them to the different platforms, optimize them so that many people can find them on the marketplace platform and then just wait for customers to buy from you through the platforms.

Also with this business model it is worth thinking about hiring someone else to do the work for you. You can outsource this work to Eastern Europe or Southeast Asia, for example. Platforms like onlinejobs.ph, Fiverr or Upwork offer help here. Also on these platforms you should convince with a variety of designs and works. Only if you upload many good designs, you will be able to earn good money on these platforms.

Blogging

Working as a blogger can have advantages. You can work from anywhere in the world, you can build a passive income and pursue your passion for writing.

To start a successful blog you first need a topic that is worth blogging about. Generally speaking, I would recommend you to blog about a topic that interests you. Because if you blog about a topic that you are not interested in at all, you will quickly lose the fun in your work and probably won't be very productive. Once you have found a topic that interests you, you should think about whether it makes sense to blog in this field. It may be that this niche is simply too small and no large amount of people will read your content. And that's exactly what we don't want right now. Our goal is to inspire readers with our articles and to make sure that readers keep coming back to us and reading our posts.

So how do we start? Once we have determined our theme, we start to work out a rough strategy. The following points should be considered when developing the strategy:

- **Platform**: Where exactly will you publish your blog? Will you publish a blog on your own website, will you blog as a guest author on someone else's website or will you use an online blogging platform such as Medium? Many bloggers choose only one of the three options. In the best case, however, you will choose all three options. You should try to get as much attention as possible by using any way you can to reach more people. So start your own website, get in touch with other bloggers who already have a wide reach, build collaborations and publish your articles on online blogging platforms. You need every reader you can find, especially in the beginning. For your own website you can use Wordpress to build your first own blog. To get to know other bloggers, I would look for Facebook groups about my blogging niche or directly contact bloggers who are in the same blogging niche. To be able to blog on platforms, you just need to create an account and then start publishing your first blog articles.

- **Length of the contents**: How long should the blog articles be? There is no fixed length for blog articles. Of course, the length of your blog article should fit the environment. For example, suppose you publish your first blog article on Medium. Most articles on Medium are estimated to be between 500 and 3000 words long. Of course there are shorter and longer blogs on the platform. If you write a blog of 200 words or more, it would be very untypical for the platform. Adapting to the platform environment is a good thing. The same is true if you cooperate with other bloggers. On your own website, however, things look a little different. You should pay close attention on your website to how your customers react to the length of the articles. Is it strange for them that the articles are very short or very long? Do they want the articles to have a different length? Is it perhaps not the length of the articles at all, but rather the content that should be improved? You should clarify all these questions for yourself before you decide on a rough length for your articles. But do not forget: You are a self-publisher. You can decide how long your articles should be. You have the artistic freedom. And if your articles are very long or very short, but are exactly the way you want them to be, it would be a shame to turn your content into something you don't like. So you should always find the balance between what you want and what the reader wants from you.

- **Types of content**: What exactly will you blog about? What kind of creative content will you use? Will you use videos? Integrate images or something else? You should think about which content is relevant for your target audience. Collect a number of topics that might be of interest to your readers and make a public poll, for example on Facebook or elsewhere, and ask your readers which topic would interest them most. You then work through the most interesting topics and wait for your readers to respond. Your readers will tell you whether they are satisfied with your content or not. Your task is then to listen to your readers and make the necessary improvements.

- **Monetization**: Next, we need to make sure that your blog actually makes you money. You can monetize your blog in many different ways. You can include affiliate links in your blog articles. These are links that lead to other people's products. For every sale made through your link, you will receive a commission. Or you can integrate links to your own products into your blog. You can also link to your own services or redirect people directly from you to your Fiverr sales page, for example.

  However, you can make money not only with products and services through your blog, but also with advertising. Google AdSense has created a unique way to make money with advertising. Google AdSense allows you to add advertising to your website. If visitors of your website see or click on the advertising, you will receive money.

  If you don't want to use Google AdSense, you can also manually sell advertising to your customers and charge them monthly for one ad space on your website.

- **Longevity**: Before you publish your blog, you should think about whether this blogging niche will be relevant for the coming years. Because longevity is very important for every entrepreneur.

Affiliate marketing

You don't necessarily have to develop products yourself and sell them to make money. You can make very good money by receiving commissions via the so-called affiliate marketing. The concept behind affiliate marketing is easy to explain. You sell other people's products and receive a commission for every sale. This commission usually ranges from a few percent up to sixty percent of the sales price. To be successful in affiliate marketing, you need interesting products and effective marketing strategies. But before you start with affiliate marketing, you should know the following. Affiliate marketing is not for everyone and there are different commission models. For example, you can sell Amazon products as an affiliate and receive a unique commission for each sale. At Amazon this commission per sale is about four percent. For example, if you sell an Amazon product that costs a hundred Euros, you would receive a commission of four Euros for each sale. So you would have to sell many hundreds of this product every month to make a living from affiliate marketing. To avoid starting from zero every month, it can be worthwhile to sell affiliate products that pay a commission every month. Especially in the software sector there are many products that pay a monthly commission as long as the customer who bought the product via your link continues to pay for the product. For example you could sell the software Clickfunnels. If people get Clickfunnels through your link, you will receive a payout every month and don't have to do anything more. If you promote such products, you will most likely be able to scale your income much faster than with products that only pay a commission once.

Of course, there are exceptions here again. For example, with luxury items. Many companies offer commissions. For example, you can also broker yachts and receive a commission for every sale. Let's assume you know someone who wants to buy a yacht. This person would be willing to spend 400,000 Euros on a yacht. Many yacht manufacturers pay ten percent as commission on each sale. You could get a commission of 40,000 Euros from a single sale. Just one or two sales per year could cover all running costs and give you a good life.

As you can see, affiliate marketing is very versatile. You should therefore carefully consider which products you want to sell.

You should start thinking about the ways in which you could sell a product. Do you already have reach or do you need to build it up first? If you already have reach, you should measure that reach. How many people can you reach and what kind of people are they? Are these people willing to buy something from you or not? What interests do these people have? If you find out that these people are interested in electronics, you could market electronic goods to them. If they have other interests, you can of course suggest other products to them. Just give it a try. You will see how your target group reacts to your posts and your product suggestions.

If you don't have reach yet, you should build up reach in order to make money with affiliate marketing. For example, you could create a Facebook group for a specific product. For example you could create a Clickfunnels Facebook group where you invite people who are interested in Clickfunnels and the topic sales funnels in general. To grow such a group, you could join other groups about this topic and post a link to your group in these groups. As soon as the group has a few hundred members, you should post interesting posts about sales funnels in this group. More and more people are becoming active in the group, commenting, linking and posting themselves. A vibrant group is a prerequisite for building affiliate revenue. Since you own the group, you can attach a post to the top of the group with a link to the software Clickfunnels and an invitation to use Clickfunnels. You will not believe how many people will click on this link and get the software. This is one of the easiest strategies to make money with affiliate marketing.

However, there are other strategies to build up reach. You could start an Instagram profile and post photos. You could build an email list and set up a regular newsletter to your contacts. Or you could offer free calls with you as an expert, where you sell software or other products to your customer. It is always important that you do not expect the customer to buy from you, but that you offer the customer added value. You could build a YouTube channel and record interesting videos every day. In your videos you could point out that there is an affiliate link in the video description where viewers can buy the software you discuss in the video.

You could also start a blog where you post interesting articles every week. These articles can be found by search engines like Google and will give you more reach. If you include affiliate links in your articles, more and more people will click on the links over time, buy the software or product and build up passive income.

It is also possible to create so-called niche pages. Many people visit Google and other search engines as a reference for their shopping list. Since many people no longer want to go to a shop to buy products, they look for these products online. You could create an online shop for the very products that people are looking for. But you don't sell the products, you just redirect the visitors of your website to platforms like Amazon. So people go to your website, click on the links to the products on your website, and they are directed to Amazon. For every purchase your website visitors make, you receive a commission. This way you can also easily build up a passive income with affiliate marketing.

Amazon Kindle Publishing

Another way to make money online is to sell e-books and paperback books through Amazon. Amazon has developed a program especially for books called Amazon Kindle Publishing. Through Amazon Kindle Publishing you can publish your books on Amazon and receive a commission for every sale. When you upload a book as a paperback, Amazon prints it for you and sends it to your customer.

To publish on Amazon Kindle, all you need is a business or freelancer status, a formatted book and a cover.

There are two ways you can make money on Amazon Kindle. You can write your own books and sell them on the platform. You can also hire other people to write books for you. These people are called ghostwriters. Ghostwriters can be hired for small money on many online platforms. However, there are also big differences in quality between different ghostwriters. Of course you don't have to hire ghostwriters, but this could be a very useful strategy because you need many books to make good money on Amazon.

The first step to starting your Amazon Kindle business is to think of a theme for a book. However, you shouldn't pick just any topic, but a topic that is profitable. Profitable topics can be found out with keyword tools, for example. One of the most popular keyword tools is for example PublisherRocket. With this tool you can analyze different niches and find out which theme is really profitable.

Once you have found a profitable topic, you should continue to find a suitable length for the book. Should your book have only a few dozen pages or maybe even many hundreds of pages? Most books published on Amazon Kindle are between 15000 and 20000 words long. I would recommend that you stay within that range. But don't worry if the book gets a bit longer or shorter. 15000 to 20000 words is only a guideline.

Once you have determined an approximate length, write down the topics you definitely want to convey in your book. I assume that you are writing a non-fiction book and that you are not interested in fiction books for the time being. Write down five ideas. These ideas should become your chapters. For each chapter you should write down some keywords. Five keywords are usually enough to create a rough structure for the book. Many things will only come up when writing the book. Don't be too perfectionist in the beginning. It is also best to determine an approximate length per chapter. That way you can make sure that you don't write too much and that you finish your book quickly.

Then start writing the book. You have a lot of work ahead of you. Try to organize your work. Usually a thousand words a day is enough to make rapid progress. You just have to work continuously and you must not give up. If you reach your personal goal every day, you will finish your book faster than you could have imagined at the beginning.

After you've written the book, it also needs to be formatted so you can upload it to Amazon Kindle. If I were you, I wouldn't format the book myself, I would have someone else do the work for me. You can get such work done on platforms like Fiverr for ten Euros or less. You don't have to pay hundreds of Euros for someone to format your book. Such sums are not necessary.

After your book has been formatted, you should send it to someone who will create the cover for your book. Kindle e-book and paperback cover designers are also available. Don't take the first one you find, but look for someone who can create professional covers and offer great value for money. You should not spend more than forty Euros on your cover. After all, we want to make profits quickly and not wait forever for the first profits to come in. This is especially true for books that you have had written by a ghostwriter.

You now have everything you need to publish your book. All you have to do now is create an account on Amazon and publish your book. Amazon will ask you to join the KDP Select program. I would highly recommend this, because you will then receive seventy percent of the revenues from e-book sales on Amazon. However, you will not be allowed to publish the e-book online on any other platform. However, you may still offer your book as a physical book on other platforms.

After your book is published, you have to market it. One of the easiest ways is to use the organic reach of Amazon. Amazon has millions of daily users. They could also become aware of your books. You just have to make sure that your book is on one of the first pages of Amazon in your niche. You do this by collecting many reviews about Amazon. You can easily get reviews by building a community, which is practically a group of people who are interested in you and your products. You can do this technically via Facebook, for example, in the form of a Facebook group. You look for people who appreciate you and your work and add them to the group. As soon as a new book of yours is published, you post a message to this group and ask them to buy the book and leave a review.

Of course there are other ways to get ratings. Amazon allows you to start a free promotion for your books once a quarter. During this time you can make your e-book available to your customers for free. They can then download the book and leave a review. This is another easy way to get ratings. Of course you are not allowed to pay people to leave reviews. Amazon does not allow this and I wouldn't do it at all if I were you, because Amazon finds out about it quickly. Build up a community and inspire other people with your content.

CHAPTER 4: Time management

Time management advice for entrepreneurs

For us entrepreneurs, time is our most important asset. Most of the time you have the feeling that time is the thing you have least of, although you need it most. This is exactly why we should try to optimize our time as much as possible and not waste it. In the following, I would like to show you five efficient rules that will help you better organize and use your time.

1. **The 2 minute rule:** Many of us love doing nothing. But doing nothing becomes a problem relatively soon, especially if you work from home. We often put off even tiny tasks and turn them into big tasks for us. This is exactly where the two minute rule comes in. If something takes less than two minutes, do it now. This strategy has helped me a lot to finally become more productive and use my time more effectively. Whenever I am faced with a task, I ask myself if I can complete the task in less than two minutes. If so, I do the task right now.

2. **Create to do lists:** To achieve your goals every day, you should create to do lists. These to do lists don't have to be very complicated, but they should list exactly what you need to do to achieve your personal goals that day. Most importantly, your daily goals must be realistic. If your goals are unrealistic, you should not develop such a list in the first

place.

To structure a to do list efficiently, you should give each task a fixed time. Divide your daily time into large time blocks and work effectively on your tasks during these blocks.

3. **Write down how much money you made:** This strategy is a mixture of a time management and productivity hack. Money can be a very good source of motivation and money helps us to better manage our time. We usually think instinctively about which decision is goal-oriented and which is not, which job earns money and which does not. However, you can also use motivation as a driving force by writing down how much money you have earned after tasks. For example, suppose you want to write a book. With a book you earn at least 2000 Euros. Your book has 40000 words. You would now know that every word you write is worth 0.05 Euros. If you wrote twenty words, you would earn 1 Euro. Try to make a game out of this and try to write as many words as possible in a time interval of for example ten minutes. At the end of the interval you will calculate how much money you have earned. Money will help you stay motivated. Always write down how much money you have earned with a certain task.

4. **Big blocks of time:** Many people try to divide their day into many small sections. However, this seems to be an effective method only for very few of us. Many small tasks put you under stress and you often spend a lot of time changing from task to task. Your own concentration also deteriorates and

your attention loses focus. Often important decisions are made hastily, which can have catastrophic consequences. Therefore it makes more sense for most of us to create large blocks of time in which we devote ourselves to certain tasks. Instead of completing twenty small tasks and entering them into our digital calendar, we can simply allow for many hours to complete these tasks. This way, we can spend more time on tasks that require more time and quickly complete those tasks that require less time. In addition, this way of planning the day reduces your own stress and you can go to bed at the end of the day with a clear conscience.

5. **No multitasking:** Multitasking is also often referred to as a widespread disease. In our everyday life we often have to complete several tasks at the same time. However, few people know that this can damage our brain, weakens our concentration and prevents us from focusing on tasks properly. By banning multitasking from your life, you manage to bring more peace into your life and give your tasks a clear structure. This will also make it easier for you to complete the tasks a second time if necessary.

However, all these tips are unimportant if you are not working continuously and doing your best to cope with tasks. Often we lack motivation or discipline and that is why we are not able to cope with tasks. However, both can be learned. Do not give up quickly and try to focus on the reason why you started the task. Do not lose sight of your goal. Because when you started your task, you were convinced of it and understood the meaning behind the task. Remember that, and you will continue to have great success in completing your task.

Also, make sure you get enough exercise and are healthy. A healthy mind always includes a healthy body. If you don't get enough sleep and eat properly, you will never be able to use your time effectively, because you will never be able to reach your full potential.

In summary, time management is more than just effectively managing your time. You should rather take a holistic view of your situation and make the changes that will allow you to work faster and more flexibly.

5 everyday distractions & how to minimize them

It is not easy to stay focused all the time. There are many distractions that could cause us problems. Because every time we get distracted, we lose precious time that we could have put into our business or that we could have used in some other way. We should always try to reduce distractions to an absolute minimum. But I also don't want you to think that every second of every day must be used. You are the master of your own time. But what you should do is try to use the time you can use productively.

What distractions are there that cost us precious time every day?

1. **Social media:** One of the biggest distractions that exists is social media. Be it Facebook, Instagram, Snapchat or

any other social networking platform. Most social networks are not relevant to your business. That's why you should try to keep the use of social media during your business to an absolute minimum. You can do this for example by storing the smartphone you normally use to access social media platforms in another room. You can also simply turn it off or give it to someone else who can't give it back to you until your working hours are over. In general, you should also consider whether you need so many profiles on social media platforms. Do you need your profiles on Twitter, Instagram, Snapchat, Facebook, WhatsApp, and many other social media platforms? In most cases, you are friends with your friends on Facebook and the other platforms are just for entertainment. Especially if you want to work from home, you should be focused, because all the responsibility is on your shoulders. You are the only person who cares about putting food on the table. You may be the only person who brings money home. So try to eliminate unnecessary distractions like social media platforms from your life as much as possible. And if you don't want to delete your profiles on social media platforms, you should at least make sure during your working hours that nothing can upset you. No mail from a friend, no push messages and no phone calls.

2. **People around you:** Please do not misunderstand me. Social contacts are extremely important, but if your social contacts no longer allow you to work actively, then this is

a problem. Many people who work from home become lazy after a certain time. This laziness should never start with you. You build up completely new circles of friends, get more and more messages via social media and before you know it, you're hardly concentrating on your own work anymore. You should try to have fixed hours every day at which you work. At this time nothing and nobody should bother you. No one can call you (except potential business clients), you don't let anyone into your workspace and just focus on your work for a while. After you have finished your work, you can still meet your friends and socialize at any time. Unfortunately, both of these things together usually work badly.

3. **Natural distractions:** There are always things around you that will distract you. Maybe the kitchen is right next to your study and you get up every few minutes to see if there is anything left to eat in the kitchen. Your own mind tries everything to distract you from your work. You must not give in to it. But maybe not only food will distract you, but your own pet, your children, other people or maybe even the weather. There are always things that can distract you. Your job is not to minimize social contacts, but to manage them properly. Explain to your children that you need some time to get work done, eat something before you work so that you don't get hungry while you work or chew gum. There is always a way if you are looking for it. Make an effort and you will find solutions.

4. **E-mails:** Another activity that can be distracting is replying to e-mails. However, this is also one of the distractions that is easiest to get out of the way. Many people answer their e-mails several times a day. Many people even try to answer them directly as soon as a new e-mail arrives in their inbox. This is exactly what you need to avoid. Set yourself clear rules when it comes to writing and answering e-mails. It's best to set two fixed times every day when you answer e-mails. However, you should not spend more time than this to answer e-mails.

5. **The own mind:** The own mind is a master of doing nothing. We love to think about things and usually do this completely unconsciously. Our mind wants to be in a free state. But when we work on tasks that do not give us pleasure and that do not allow our mind to be free, then our mind will try to keep us from these tasks. It downright encourages us not to be productive. You should train your mind that it loves to handle tasks because at the end of the work process there is a reward waiting. This could be something sweet or just a relaxing evening in front of the TV. Give your mind something to look forward to. Because then it will actively try to reach this state quickly.

Discipline and motivation

Discipline and motivation are driving forces in our lives. Both terms are often confused or used as synonyms. Motivation and discipline could hardly be more different. Motivation is temporary and cannot be learned. Discipline is not temporary, but it can be learned. Motivation is like a push that helps the body to get everything out of itself, while discipline is the body that you have trained for years.

To become more disciplined, you should first of all get to know yourself better. Because most of us don't know what we're capable of. Most of the time we can do much more than we think, but we don't have enough confidence in ourselves. Be honest with yourself. Are you honest with yourself or are you just trying to give this impression? Then set yourself a goal for the next twenty-four hours. That goal should take everything from you. For example, you could set yourself the goal of running thirty kilometers in one day. Many people think they could never do that, but many people do it because they try and are disciplined. In this experiment you should go to your personal limits. This will not only show you that you can achieve more than you think you can, it will also help you to move forward in life. Other strategies for becoming more disciplined include caring for a living animal. Many such experiments were conducted in the USA in the 1980s. Back then, many young children had to look after an animal for a month, usually a chick. They had to take care of the chick, feed it and bring it back after a month. Surprisingly, most of the children brought the chicks back completely unharmed, because they had learned to take responsibility during this time. And once you have taken responsibility for other people or creatures, it will be easier for you to take responsibility for yourself.

Another way to improve your discipline is to do a small task every day. For example to go ten minutes jogging, write a diary entry or record a video every day. By thinking about a daily task and completing it, you will realize how disciplined you have to be to complete only small tasks each day. At some point, you won't do just one task a day, but two tasks, then three, and so on. Productivity and discipline is based on regularity.

Motivation as opposed to discipline is something very temporary. Sometimes the motivation is there and sometimes it is not. It is not enough to just watch a motivational video every morning. You need a motivation that comes from deep inside you. This motivation should make you jump out of bed every morning. The easiest way to find that motivation is to find your perfect life. If it is possible for you to travel the world, then by all means do so. Somewhere in the world you will find a place that you like so much that you want to stay there. Once you have found such a place, you will get up every morning with the same motivation. And that kind of motivation won't leave you so quickly.

If you do not have the possibility to travel, it is advisable to visualize your goals. Take a big piece of cardboard and stick on it photos of dreams you have and photos of people who are very important to you. This is exactly what you are working for. Hang up this cardboard in a place where you can always see it. And if one day you are not so motivated to work, just look at the cardboard with all the photos and you know again what you are working for every day. But visualizing goals can work well in other cases as well. For example, you can hang a photo of a person with a dream body next to the mirror, so that every time you look in the mirror, you'll remember that you want to look like that. The same concept also works for your company's income. For example, you can write a sum of money on a piece of paper that you really want to earn this year. While you are working, you put the paper in a place where you can see it at any time. This way you stay motivated and always keep an eye on your goals.

And if these strategies work for you, you can of course use any other strategy that comes to mind. If something motivates you to work harder, use it as your source of motivation.

However, you can motivate yourself not only by pure thought, but also by a taste of what you might soon have. For example, you could spend a few days every year in a luxury hotel, just to motivate you to become more successful. Or you could buy an expensive watch, which would give you a daily foretaste of what you could expect at the end of your journey.

Whatever strategy you choose, always try to combine motivation with discipline. Train your discipline and try to find something that motivates you. Once you have done both of these things, you should start to work. Focus on your discipline. And if your discipline fails one day, you should use motivation as an extra boost to get ahead.

Another tip I would like to give you at the end of this book is not to feel sorry for yourself. Work hard and don't look back too much. A night shift won't steal years of your life and a little stress won't throw you off track. The important thing is that you can handle stress. Therefore, you should find a balance to your entrepreneurial activity. Be it football, painting, listening to music or whatever.

Life is not only about work. Make your work area as comfortable as possible and try to bring yourself in the best possible position, then you will be successful.

Closing words

We really looked at a lot of different concepts here in this book and I hope that you were able to take something for yourself.

Working from home can really bring a lot of freedom that you don't want to lose so quickly. You will have the opportunity to work whenever you want, you don't have to listen to anyone else, you don't have to leave home and you can earn very good money.

It is comfortable and easy to work for someone else. However, the true freedom to work from wherever you want is outweighed by no money in the world. And don't forget: if you earn good money, you can take a holiday whenever you want. No other person will ever be able to tell you when to leave the hotel and take the next flight home.

Even if times get tough, there is no reason to give up. No successful entrepreneur has not failed. Failure is part of the learning process. You just have to get up quickly and keep going. Then nothing can happen to you.

Use this book as a guide and return from time to time to places in this book that have particularly interested you. Mark the passages you found particularly important and form your own opinion about everything.

You now have all the necessary skills to start your own business and work from home. Now it's time for the implementation.

I wish you success on your journey.

Imprint

Uwe Sawinski

Hubertusstrasse 157

44577 Castrop-Rauxel

Germany

www.ingramcontent.com/pod-product-compliance
Lightning Source LLC
Chambersburg PA
CBHW020602220526
45463CB00006B/2408